Becoming What You Want to See in the World

THE ART OF JOYFUL LIVING

by
Mary Claire O'Neal

River Birch
PUBLISHING ™
Lexington, KY

River Birch
PUBLISHING ™

Published by:
River Birch Publishing, LLC
P.O. Box 23198
Lexington, KY 40523-3198

Book Design: Jamie O'Neal
Cover/Interior Art: Nick Henderson/Digital Vision/Getty Images
Quotation page 15: courtesy of the American Foundation for the Blind,
Helen Keller Archives

Manufactured in the United States of America

Library of Congress Control Number: 2005909347

Publisher's Cataloging Data:

O'Neal, Mary Claire
Becoming what you want to see in the world : the art of joyful living / Mary
Claire O'Neal.

104 p. ; 21.6 cm.

Includes bibliographical references
ISBN: 0-9772566-0-X
ISBN (13): 978-0-9772566-0-0

1. Personal development. 2. Personal growth. 3. Communication I. Title.
158.1—dc22

CONTENTS

ACKNOWLEDGMENTS

I want thank my dear husband, Cam, for his loving help in editing and proofing this book and his unending support throughout the process. I am very grateful to my sister, Jamie, for the generous and loving gift of her professionalism and creativity in the design and layout of this book. I want to express my thanks and gratitude to my dear friend, Lea, who has been, in so many ways, such a loving inspiration in my life. I am grateful to my mother and father for their loving encouragement of my dreams and for always desiring to see me happy. I am also very grateful to my extended family of friends whose loving thoughts helped me in the flow of this project. Many thanks to all those who contributed to this book with their loving help. I am very grateful for the loving Teacher of my soul (who gives me a nudge off the cliff when I need it). I am so thankful and grateful for the peace that experiencing and living love brings to my heart.

INTRODUCTION

I used to think that attaining happiness and fulfillment was just an illusion—a cosmic joke. I really thought that humanity was given this intense desire to find meaning and joy in daily life, but, like Don Quixote, we were striving for something unattainable, an impossible dream. A sad way to think? Yes, *because it wasn't true,* and it made me a cynical, unhappy person.

It had a profound effect on me when a dear friend sat me down one day and said, "You are here to be happy and fulfilled, and you can attain it. You can be what you want to see more of in the world." That was many years ago, and he was absolutely right. I am writing this book to relay the same message. You have picked up this book because either you have hopes that you can find *more* happiness or that you already know in your heart that my friend's statement is true.

We all have a mountain to climb—our path in life. For most people the desired path is happiness, fulfillment, and love. Whatever you label it, it is *your* journey, *your* path, and only you can decide what works best for you. There are many ways to travel up a mountain. This book will give you principles and practical tools for helping make the hike more joyful, and easier, hopefully, but *what is offered here is not the only way.* I *will* say, however, that these principles and tools have worked for me and many others. But don't take my word for it! The only way you will know is to try out these approaches, and see if they work for *you.* But like any set of tools, if they stay in the toolbox and are not used, they are useless.

My deepest desire in writing this book is that you will find it useful on your journey of happiness and love, becoming what you want to see more of in the world. With hope in my heart and the willingness to keep "hiking," I discovered that life can be easier, more joyful, more loving, and more fulfilling.

I have never known anyone who has said to me, "I've got just about all the happiness and love I can stand! No more joy for me, thank you!" Whether you have picked up this book because you feel a bit overwhelmed by your schedule, you are in a slump, you are experiencing some bumps in the road in your interactions with others, you feel things are a bit chaotic, or you want to create a more happy, peaceful and meaningful life for yourself in general, my hope is that you find this book helpful and practical on your path.

Mary Claire O'Neal

July 4, 2005

CHAPTER 1

HAPPINESS IS RIGHT NOW

Joy is not in things, it is in us.
–Benjamin Franklin–

Do you believe that consistent happiness is an elusive thing? All of us have had experiences or moments of happiness in our lives that tell us happiness exists and it *is* possible. But do you believe that experiencing happiness everyday is possible? Do you find yourself thinking that happiness is something that happens in the future—maybe when you get this much money or that relationship?

Our experience of happiness comes from within us. This truth is nothing new, but it is so easily forgotten in our day-to-day living.

Have you ever looked to a relationship(s) to make you happy? I have, but it wasn't until I discovered that I had to become happy and fulfilled *first* that I started creating relationships with others that were happy and fulfilling

We are all here to be happy, consistently happy. Sure, we will all have our "bumps in the road," times or moments of pain or feeling down. What I mean by *consistent happiness* is that everyday there are many, many opportunities for joy, and finding those moments and opportunities is what this book is about.

Happiness is not something that just "lucky" people are blessed with. Happiness is a *focus of mind,* a way of perceiving experience, a way of *living. Happiness begins right now, within you, and it is a process.*

CHAPTER 2

BEGIN WHERE YOU ARE

People are about as happy as they make up
their minds to be.
—Abraham Lincoln—

Our minds are so dynamic that they are almost constantly engaged in thought and a monologue of self-talk. Our self-talk or monologue is composed of perceptions and feelings created by how we think and what we think about. Our *thoughts* come from our experiences and also from our *beliefs* about ourselves and our world. This internal monologue of thoughts and self-talk is *intrapersonal* communication.

What do you communicate to yourself moment to moment? This intrapersonal communication reflects your baseline relationship with happiness in your life. Throughout my twenties and into my thirties, I experienced bouts with feeling depressed. It was a depression created by what I thought about me and my world. Many of my perceptions were distorted and not based on realistic assessments. We all have some distortions in our perceptual reality. Growing up in the world can give us messages in different ways that we are not enough, and, for the most part, those messages are unintentional. Our perceptions of those messages, however, if we buy into them, become *beliefs* that form the foundation of our experience.

As I mentioned earlier, our self-talk, our intrapersonal communication, is a reflection of what we think, perceive and believe. Because this inner monologue is running through our minds constantly, we learn to ignore it much of the time. The problem with that is we no longer *hear* the thoughts that are profoundly affecting our lives on a daily basis. If we are unaware of what is being communicated within us, the foundation of how we are perceiving ourselves and our world is coming from an unconscious level. And if we heard what was going through our heads, we may no longer agree with some of the stuff that we are constantly telling ourselves.

As long as we are *unaware* of these thoughts that are affecting our lives so profoundly, it is difficult to remove obstacles in our path to happiness and fulfillment or to reinforce those positive, life-affirming thoughts that help us. So, with that in mind, what are we saying to ourselves at any given time? The first step is to start hearing it again, and what follows is an exercise to help with that.

TOOL #1

Self-Monitoring

*In the coming weeks, monitor your self-talk. This is an ongoing activity to continue long after you have finished reading this book. When you hear positive affirming thoughts, mentally make a note of them, and jot them down. They are probably affecting your life in good and healthy ways. When you hear a limiting, fearful or negative thought, replace it **in that moment** with a more healthy, positive thought. Here is an example:*

"I can't get up in front of the group at the meeting. I'll just blank out."

You could replace this thought with something like:

"It's okay. I can get up and speak at the meeting. I will prepare ahead of time, and I will know what I am going to say. I will have notes on cards to help me if I need it. I will be fine. I can do this."

The important thing to remember is to replace those negative, fearful and defeating thoughts when you hear them. Trying to push the thought out of your mind without replacing it with something else just makes it harder to think about anything other than the original thought. That resistance also gives that negative thought more focus and energy in your life. If I ask you not to think of a big, sticky, rich piece of chocolate cake, what are you thinking of? Your mouth might already be watering!

*So replace limiting, fearful or negative thoughts with positive, affirming thoughts. This may sound simplistic, but it works! Monitoring your self-talk is Tool #1 for your toolbox. Over and over again in my life, I have found that the simplest things are usually the most profound. The profundity comes in **living** those simple principles.*

To take this process a little further, what do you do with those negative thoughts that keep coming back time and time again even after you have worked at replacing them? Those persistent thoughts can be rooted in a belief or past experience that you may not have identified yet. So, simply replacing them a few times may not be enough. It may be a very old belief that has been with you most of your life. That may take longer to replace with a new way of thinking and behaving.

Sometimes looking at *why* you are having a thought is helpful. Where is it coming from? A dialogue with myself is the easiest and fastest way I know of to find out where a thought is coming from. I know that I am not happy if I am holding resentments or anger toward others or myself. Let's say you just noticed an isolated, negative thought about someone you know and haven't seen for a long time. Where in the heck did that come from?

Try approaching a conversation with yourself like you are conversing with a dear friend:

Why are you having a negative thought about Lydia? Where did that come from?

She wasn't very nice to me.

What do you mean, she wasn't very nice?

She's been unkind.

How has she been unkind to you?

She said some sarcastic things, making fun of me in front of friends.

Did that hurt you?

Yes.

When did this happen?

About two or three years ago.

You're still resenting her for that after all this time?

I didn't know that I was. I don't think about her much.

It seems, though, that this thought is telling you that it is something that needs attention.

I don't want to hold onto this any longer, because I am not happy with thoughts like this.

So, what is to be done?

She needs to be forgiven.

Forgiven for saying those things?

Yes.

Every time she comes into your mind, think the best of her. Say, to yourself: "Lydia, I know that you would not intend to hurt my feelings. You are probably completely unaware of the effects your words had on me. I want to let go of this. I forgive you, and I forgive myself for feeling anger toward you."

But what if she did intend to hurt me?

That's not likely, but even if she did, do you want these thoughts to continue to make you unhappy because you have not forgiven her?

No, I don't like the way it feels.

So, you have nothing to lose but feelings that make you unhappy, and everything to gain in their place—peace and happiness.

It's a deal.

CHAPTER 3

THE PHYSICS OF HAPPINESS
AND FULFILLMENT

"No pessimist ever discovered the secret of the stars,
or sailed to an uncharted land, or opened a new doorway
for the human spirit."

–Helen Keller–

When you turn on a news broadcast, what do you hear? When you open a newspaper, what types of stories are in the majority? In this time of change and transition in our world, it's more of a challenge to find balance in our thoughts and perceptions and maintain a positive state of mind. Unfortunately, the focus, especially in our media, is primarily on the negative, what is not working in our world (with the dramatic emphasized) instead of what *is* working. This contributes strongly to a perception that the world is *full* of violence, corruption and suffering. Now, don't get me wrong, those things *are* in our world, and it is important that we know about them so we are more aware and may choose to help in our own ways—whether it be contributing clothing for a local family whose house burned, writing letters to our governmental representatives or leaders, or prayer. But the perceptual problem comes in when the focus is *mainly* on what is *wrong or not working*.

The truth is, there are just as many, if not more, things working in our world that we never hear about—positive stories of happiness, victory, fulfillment, healing, and love. There are many books out there that have been put together to share collections of positive stories. These wonderful experiences are happening all around us, all the time. If you review your life, you may have some stories of your own experiences for your happiness archive, and through the perception of the eyes of love, you will have many, many more experiences!

Earlier in my adult life I would have thought that this type of thinking was only wishful or Pollyannish, but my negative focus and cynicism kept me from seeing what was all around me. This is physics. I'll explain later.

TOOL #2

News Fast

*For about 30 days, try to limit your focus on the news to either one 30-minute news broadcast per day **or** only 30 minutes of reading the newspaper per day. Also try not to start your day with the news first thing. My husband and I used to be news junkies—tuning into the 24-hour cable news channels frequently. We found that when we tried this exercise for a month and limited our exposure to the media, we were less stressed and anxious and more focused in positive ways. Also, the time we spent in watching unending news cycles and reading the news, we were able to use in more enjoyable, constructive ways.*

If just living in the world and hearing the information coming at us can create an imbalance in our perception of reality, how do we re-create a balance in our thinking and, thereby, our perceptions? **By focusing on what is working!** Focus on the positive. Again, sounds simplistic? The *living* of it changes lives.

Creating that positive focus in our minds is not something that we do just once, and it stays a done deal. That positive focus, and the happiness that results from it, is a *process* (there's that word again), and it unfolds moment to moment. It works like self-esteem, which is also a process. You don't achieve a healthy level of self-esteem (which is also a part of experiencing happiness and fulfillment) and never have to do anything more to maintain it. The inevitable bumps in the road make it necessary to work on maintaining it. Happiness is not an automatic thing that happens to just those who are blessed or lucky. Happiness and fulfillment require awareness, focus and energy in order to maintain them in our lives.

At the end of this chapter will be a tool called the Joy Journal. Keeping this journal has been one of the most powerful tools in helping me create balance in my thoughts and perceptions. People who have taken my workshops and tried the Joy Journal have written to me and let me know that they, too, found it to be an easy and effective tool for positive transformation. It is very simple—all entries must be positive in nature. And it works.

Many years ago when I started keeping my Joy Journal, I had bouts with feeling down or what I think of now (when I look back) as cognitive depression—depressions that I created through my negative self-talk, thoughts, and perceptions of myself and the world. Many years ago when I first sat down to write in my Joy Journal, I could think of nothing positive to write down or feel happy about. How sad. I sat there for ten minutes with the first page of my notebook blank.

Finally the thought came to me, "You got up this morning, that's something." And I wrote it down. Then the thought, "I took a hot bath this morning, and it made me feel good all over." And I wrote that down. Then I thought, "These entries aren't significant enough to put in my journal." My next thought was, "Of course they are! My life is made up of these moments, and that is where my happiness is!" This was one of the most inspired moments of my life.

Through the years, I have learned the truth of that realization. After keeping my journal for about three weeks, I started noticing changes in the way I experienced my days, my moments, my life. Keeping this journal is one of the easiest and most powerful things I have ever done. It has a cumulative effect and helps restructure thinking and re-create balance.

But there is even more gravy! This daily focus not only helps you see what works and what is joyful and positive that has been right there in front of you all along, it helps you draw more positive experiences to you, as well.

Many years ago, after I had been doing the Joy Journal for a couple of months, I was explaining it to a dear friend. I told him how I was able to turn my life around and really experience more and more happiness and fulfillment. I told him that it also seemed that my awareness in doing this journal multiplied the positive, happy experiences in my life.

His reply was, "It's the physics of happiness or the 'nature' of happiness."

"Physics?" I replied incredulously.

"What you focus on creates an affinity for that in your life. When you meet someone who you really like, it's because the *similarities* you share with that person make them attractive to you. You think of all the things you have in common." He went on to tell me a story to further illustrate his point.

"I have a friend named Elwood who drives a small blue truck. Now, before I met Elwood, I never noticed small blue trucks. Now I see them everywhere. They were always there, I just never saw them."

I could remember times in my life when I had learned a new word, for example, and then started seeing it in print everywhere. Your awareness is more open to that which you are focused on and has meaning for you and draws more of the same to you. That certainly was the way my Joy Journal was working.

This same idea, however, works both ways. If you are focused on the negative, guess what?

Even now, I still do my Joy Journal fairly regularly—especially when I am a little down or experience one of those inevitable bumps in the road. It's kind of an ongoing dialogue with myself—celebrating and re-creating my life. It's the physics of happiness.

TOOL #3

The Joy Journal

Before you do the Joy Journal worksheet at the end of this chapter, here are a few practical tips:

- *Doing this journal only need take about five to ten minutes a day. You can spend more time, if you wish, but this exercise can be done in about five to ten minutes.*

- *When you start your journal, find the kind of notebook that will be most useful or enjoyable for you. You might want to use a little notebook for your pocket or purse, so you can write things down throughout your day, or you might want something more elaborate. I like to use journals from the bookstore that are decorated with colorful images that are visually pleasing to me.*

- *I find that writing in my journal before I go to bed can be a great way to complete the day. It gives me an opportunity to review the good things throughout the day and to celebrate them and be grateful for them. I have also found that first thing in the morning can be a good time, if you can remember the details from the day before.*

- *Attaching your journal writing to an activity you do everyday (like before going to bed or after you brush your teeth in the morning) helps in staying consistent with it. I sit down and sip a glass of lemon water in the morning, and that time works really well for writing in my journal.*

- *Even though consistency is important, if you miss a day or two, just pick it back up again on the next day.*

The Joy Journal Worksheet

There are many different types of entries you can make in your joy journal, but they all must have one thing in common: **All entries must be positive in nature.** *Here are some examples of the types of entries you can make: successes, moments of laughter and joy, victories, appreciation of beauty, giving thanks and gratitude, enjoyable activities, little (and big) miracles, love in its many forms.* **In short, a joy journal entry is in recognition of any experience that uplifts, inspires, or brings happiness and fulfillment.** *No drama, pain or pathos. In this journal write about a difficult experience* **only** *if you are able to see it as a gift and give thanks for it.*

Below are listed some ideas for the types of entries for your joy journal with space for you to fill them in. Try to write down examples in your own life that fit some of the different types of entries listed here. If you can't think of one for a particular category, just pass on it and go on to the next. The purpose for the categories listed below is to illustrate some of the many different types of entries that may come to you when you write in your journal.

Positive observations:

Love in its many forms:

Thankfulness and gratitude:

Pat-yourself-on-the-back:

Health and happiness:

Things, experiences or opportunities that you have asked for, or prayed for and received:

Fun stuff and laughter:

Successes:

Little miracles (and big ones, too!)

When you start your Joy Journal, you won't need to write down the different categories listed here, and you will probably not be writing that many different kinds of entries everyday. This is just a worksheet to start the flow. When you actually write in your journal, just begin writing about all of your positive observations and experiences from your day.

Here is a typical excerpt from my Joy Journal:

July 3

- *The hearty hibiscus in the yard is displaying huge, pink blooms today! They are stunningly beautiful! I am so grateful to Suzie for her loving help with my gardening this year.*

- *My foot is healing nicely from the break a couple of months ago. I was able to take one of my 30-minute walks today. Yes!*

- *On my walk I noticed how green and beautiful my surroundings were. Kentucky reminds me of Scotland's beauty every day!*

- *I am so grateful for my loving husband. He is an amazing gift in my life.*

- *I was looking for some notes for my work and managed to go right to them. That was a pleasant surprise.*

- *I am grateful for the warm companionship of our sweet cat, Willie. He was playful today (like he was as a kitten) and made me laugh with his antics.*

- *I got all the items on my checklist accomplished. That's satisfying.*

- *My mother called today, and it was fun just chatting with her.*

- *We had a great time with our friends this past weekend. Lots of laughter!*

At first your entries may be few in number. That's fine and typical for most people. They will probably increase in number within a few days or a week. You may have a day in which you just want to take stock of the things you are grateful for—which is a very powerful focus.

*Remember that with this journal, or anything that is new in our lives, **progress comes in steps.***

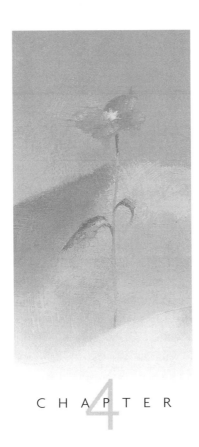

C H A P T E R 4

THE POWER OF GRATITUDE

Wake at dawn with a winged heart and give thanks
for another day of loving.
–Kahlil Gibran–

Gratitude is one of the most powerful states of mind and heart that creates happiness—consistent happiness. Feeling gratitude for what I already have has been an amazing and loving way for me to sustain happiness.

Expressing gratitude to others is a way of acknowledging, aloud, the gifts that have come to us in our lives through others. What we express gratitude for can be a small gesture or a large gift, it doesn't matter. Acknowledging others brings them joy, and it can bring us joy for *giving* that acknowledgement.

I love receiving the wonderful gifts of this abundant universe, and I also love giving. They both make me happy. One of the most powerful gifts I can give another person is grateful recognition. It's good to pass it around!

You may find in your Joy Journal that many of your entries involve being grateful. That is a perfect place to make a point of expressing gratitude. I have also found that by expressing gratitude to the Divine (God, Creator, Universe. . .) within my stream of thoughts throughout the day, I acknowledge and more richly experience the love that is constantly pouring into my life, bringing me happiness.

Here are only a few of the many ways you can experience and express gratitude:

- Look around you and be grateful for what you have.

- Express gratitude to your spouse or partner, if you have one. Be specific about what he or she does, no matter how small, that makes you happy or makes your life easier.

- Express gratitude to your friends and family for the love they bring into your life.

- Write (in your Joy Journal) about the moments of happiness in your day that you are grateful for.

- Be grateful for the income or prosperity in your life.

- Express gratitude to the Divine for the good things you experience and that come into your life.

- Express gratitude to your pets for the love and happiness they bring to you.

- Acknowledge a kind gesture or action from another.

- Be grateful to yourself for making a good choice or using wisdom.

- Express gratitude to coworkers or colleagues for their help or consideration.

Find ways to be in a grateful frame of mind for something that may have been difficult for you but brought you gifts of awareness or to new and joyful doorways in your life.

There are unlimited ways to think grateful thoughts and express gratitude!

Have you ever known someone who, no matter what he or she has, is constantly striving for more—focusing on what is lacking? For instance, instead of appreciating the comfortable and dependable car he or she is driving, there is discontent because the car doesn't have all the wanted luxuries? Constantly striving for more without taking stock and being grateful for the good things already in one's life makes happiness elusive. It is very difficult to be consistently happy or at peace with that kind of never-ending longing.

Stop and smell the roses and be grateful for them!

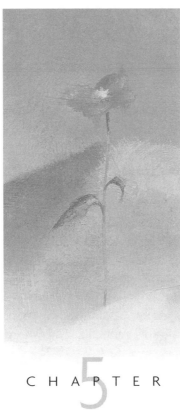

CHAPTER 5

WHAT ARE YOUR CARROTS?

Everything that I understand, I understand
only because I love.
—Leo Tolstoy—

"What makes you happy?" That question was asked of me years ago, and I didn't readily have an answer. That was the problem. If I didn't know what made me happy, how could I create that focus and state of being for myself? How could I plan goals if I didn't know where I wanted to go? When considering happiness and joy in my life, *love* is always in there somewhere. When I ask other people what brings them joy, love is always present in their answers. Think about it. Does taking walks make you happy? Why? Is it because it's an activity that you love and, therefore, brings you joy? Sure. But maybe it's an activity that you have to push yourself to do, and when you walk you feel so much better physically. You know it is helping your heart, bringing down your blood pressure, reducing your cholesterol, etc. So even though you have to make yourself take walks, love is a part of this too, because you are loving yourself and your body enough to take care of it. And you *love* the way it makes you feel.

I have also found that other joys can arise from an activity of love like taking a walk—my spirits being lifted by the sunshine, enjoyment of the beauty of the flowers in yards that I pass, and a positive mental focus with thoughts of gratefulness in the silence.

There are so many different experiences and expressions of love. Here are only a few:

- The love for and of a spouse or partner.

- The love of doing something that you are good at or brings you joy.

- The love for and of friends.

- The love for and of family.

- The love of learning new things.

- The love of the beauty of nature and the Earth.

- The love of playfulness and humor.

- The love of animals.

- The love of our spiritual nature.

- The love of God, Creator, the Universe. . .

If you have been doing the Joy Journal, then you may already know of some happiness carrots in your life.

What is a carrot? An orange root vegetable packed full of vitamin A. But symbolically what is a carrot? *A motivator.* Something we dangle in front of our noses to get us moving.

As an example, for years a big carrot for me was finding a fulfilling, happy relationship with a loving, compassionate man. ***But the carrots by themselves are not what bring us the happiness.*** I had been through enough relationships to finally figure out that relationships couldn't bring me happiness if I wasn't creating it for myself. But what that carrot *motivated me to do* was to learn how to be happier and more fulfilled myself so that I would find someone *like me*. I finally "got it" that I had to bring my loving and happy self to a relationship with another loving and happy self. Like attracts like. And that's how it worked.

The Joy Journal is an opportunity to see the joy in our lives, to see what is working, to see how blessed we really are and to be thankful. With that comes an awareness in our hearts of more of those experiences that make us happy. And with *that* comes an awareness of *what* we want more of in our lives.

The next tool (at the end of this chapter) is called the Personal Carrot Inventory. This will give you an opportunity to make a list or inventory of those joyful experiences and things in your life that you love and want to focus on and create goals for, so that you can experience more and more joy and fulfillment. It is also an important step in being able to create more balance by fitting in the time for those experiences that feed you, so you have more energy for yourself and others.

TOOL #4

The Personal Carrot Inventory

What are your favorite leisure activities?

*What were your favorite subjects in school
(any level—elementary to college)?*

What is your favorite movie(s)?

Favorite music?

Favorite vacation?

*Who is a role model for you
(someone you admire who inspires you)?*

Why?

What is/was your favorite work experience?

List two different happy memories.

What are the characteristics or qualities you look for in a best friend, lover or partner?

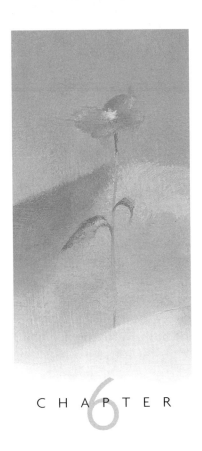

CHAPTER 6

CARROT CAVEATS

Look twice before you leap.

–Charlotte Brontë–

Following one's heart is important in finding happiness and your carrots in life, but there is a perspective of *balance* that needs to be nurtured in deciding what action to take and when to take it. For instance, you may realize that you would experience happiness by using your gift (and joy) of writing to write a novel, or you may want to use your talent for teaching to devote your time to teaching workshops. Don't quit your day job until you are able to create adequate income from your writing or teaching. You may decide to keep it as a fulfilling sideline that brings an important balance to your life.

Taking baby steps is what works for most people in making their dreams come true. I know people who have prioritized their lives so that they spend some time on the weekends or in the morning before work developing or creating their dreams. I did that with this book, and although it took me longer than it would have if I'd been able to sit down and only write, it is now a reality.

Another carrot caveat is to look down the road at what making certain choices for happiness now will bring you later.

If, for instance, I decide that life is short and that to enjoy the experience of life to the fullest I will eat *all* the foods I really love and enjoy, well, down the road, this may bring me an unhappy outcome. My life being enjoyed to it's "fullest" may end up being a very short one!

Looking at the effects our choices for happiness may have on *others* is an important part of that balance in perspective, as well. I have seen those who follow their desire for happiness in the moment without thinking through the possible effects of their actions, and they create pain in their lives that wasn't worth the original choice or experience. Always seek to do no harm. Before making a choice, if it involves others, negotiation is important to keep in mind.

Our hearts are important indicators of where our happiness lies, but we also have been given brains to look at our choices and to consider the effects of those choices. Our free will, when balanced with wisdom, discernment and love, will help us *stay* on a path of happiness.

CHAPTER 7

WHAT'S YOUR VISION?

The ancestor of every action is a thought.
–Ralph Waldo Emerson–

By now, you probably have some ideas of those joyful experiences that you want more of in your life. Where do you go from here? Creating a vision for what you truly want is a very helpful and powerful first step to bring a dream into reality. Vision gives a direction, a focus for bringing more joy and happiness into your life. Look over your Carrot Inventory and use some of the ideas you wrote down there to complete the next worksheet.

TOOL #5

Personal Vision Worksheet

Find a quiet place and set aside some time to reflect and ask yourself these questions, making notes below:

What do I really want?

What makes me happy?

I want to be:

"Happy," "more loving," "prosperous," "a better communicator," are just a few examples.

I want to do:

"Play the piano," "take walks everyday," "read more,"
"write an article," "eat healthy foods," are some examples.

I want to have:

"Confidence in _____," "more friendships,"
"a dependable car," "more balance in my life,"
"a pet," are just a few examples.

Your answers from your Personal Vision Worksheet will give you the basic information to write your vision statement(s).

Here is an example of one of my vision statements that I wrote years ago when I first started teaching workshops:

I love to teach, and I want to share what I have learned. I want to share practical tools that have worked for me that might help others in day-to-day living. Doing this makes me happy, and I want to create more opportunities for this in my life.

In this book, there are no rules for the construction of your vision statement. It just needs to articulate what you want in your heart—**with your highest and best intent.** It is helpful, however, to also have a statement in it that will get you moving toward that vision. I committed myself to action by stating my intention, ". . .and I want to create more opportunities for this in my life."

Here is another example of a very simple vision statement:

I really love reading. It relaxes me and refreshes my mind. I want to create some time in my life to read for enjoyment and relaxation.

Can you see how easily you can create goals from these vision statements? The nuts and bolts for taking action will be in the next chapter. This chapter is about your dreams—big ones and little ones. It's about becoming more specific about what you want and writing down what you love and want more of, so that you can increase the experiences that make you feel happiness and joy.

TOOL #5

Vision Statement

Use the space provided here and on page 104 to draft your vision statement. Make it simple but still expressing your highest intent. You may have more than one vision statement in mind, and that's great. Try, however, to focus on just one for now, so that you don't take on too much at one time. Once you are experiencing success with this one, then introduce another.

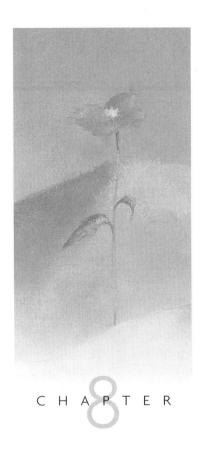

CHAPTER 8

FEAR OF THE UNKNOWN

The greatest mistake a person can make
is to be afraid of making one.
—Elbert Hubbard—

Whenever we introduce something new into our lives, we are dealing with what appears to us as the unknown. What I have discovered is that if it is something I want because it makes me happy, then it is not an unknown to me. There is something inside me that "knows" it already, at least the essence of it, because I have an affinity for it. It allows the use of a part of me that wants to experience that creativity or whatever it happens to be. Activities that I know make me happy can also lead me to something else that makes me happy and then something else that I may never have dreamed of.

I'd like to tell you a story about fear of the unknown, from the only way I can really know how this works, from my personal experience. Years ago when I had about a year left in completing my undergraduate degree, I realized that I needed to do something about my shyness. I was rather reclusive, and it was difficult for me to talk to people. I knew that if I wanted to be effective in my life and the world, I needed to get over this shyness.

I decided to enroll in an introductory acting class to fulfill an elective requirement and to possibly help me overcome my shyness. I was terrified, and at the same time, there was something that really interested me in acting. The class was small, and we did theater games almost every day. The teacher was one of those wonderful teachers who knew how to take things in baby steps so as not to overwhelm his students. I am sure that he knew why I had enrolled (just observing my body language tipped him off pretty easily). I was a little challenged some days, a little fearful, but each day progressed in steps I could handle. I *loved* the class.

One day our acting teacher announced that, as a requirement for the course, everyone in the class must audition for the main stage production. I was terrified, and after class asked him why he was requiring it. He explained that he would be remiss as a teacher to not have us experience that *process* (so that it would not be an unknown to us) should we ever decide that we would like to try acting in a play. I understood his reason, but I was still terrified.

I checked out a copy of the script and was so nervous that I read through the play about four or five times the night before the audition. I wanted to be familiar with the lines so that I wouldn't stumble when reading them the next day. I went to the audition, and we were allowed to watch everyone read the various parts. I was sitting there marveling at how wonderful everyone was—so polished and poised in reading the various roles. It made me feel so secure and happy, because I knew there was *no way* I would be cast in a role!

It was my turn to get up. I read a couple of different roles with several people. I was thanked, and I went home. I was feeling great on my way home, because I had done something that I really was afraid of and found out that I didn't turn to dust—that it wasn't as scary as I had thought it would be.

The next afternoon, posted on the entrance door to the acting class was the cast list from the auditions. I went down the list, and to my absolute horror, I had been cast in the romantic lead! I immediately went to the acting teacher's office and told him, tearfully, "I can't do this. There were so many people who auditioned better than I did. You won't have any problems filling this role. I just can't do this."

He looked at me and said, "If you want to pass this course, you *will* do it."

I was terrified, but I didn't have a choice if I wanted to keep my good academic standing and grade point average. I went to rehearsals every night, and even though I was scared, I enjoyed them. Working on a character with other actors was really fun. I enjoyed the nuances that would appear in my character and other characters in the rehearsal *process*. I loved the process.

But the product was another story. Even though I was enjoying the process in rehearsals, that specter of opening night was in the back of my mind. It was like getting on a roller coaster. Once you buy your ticket, get in the car, and they put the bar down, you are there until the end of the ride. For me the terrifying plunge was opening night, because I knew that I was going to die.

On opening night I was standing backstage waiting for my cue, and I was shaking. My legs felt like jello. My stomach felt very queasy. My breathing was fast and shallow. I was about to walk out on stage and die—an improvisation that was not written into the script.

It came time for me to walk out on stage. I walked into the bright light and stood on my mark waiting the few seconds before I was to say my first line. I remember very clearly to this day what went through my mind in those few seconds: *When I open my mouth to say my first line, there are two options available to me at this point, 1) nothing will come out, or 2) I'm going to throw up.*

I absolutely knew those were the options. When we got to the place in the dialogue where I was to say my first line, the first word came out of my mouth very tentatively, then the second, third, fourth…and then I finished the sentence. *After that point, you couldn't keep me off a stage!* I loved it once I found out I could do it without turning to dust. Sure, I experienced some nervousness after that, but that's a part of it. It quickly got easier and easier. I loved acting so much that I took more and more theater classes before graduating. I was using a part of my creativity that really fulfilled me and brought me a lot of joy. When I heard about an audition in New York, I made an appointment, went to it, and was hired for my first professional acting job. I acted professionally for about 12 years.

This story is about baby steps with a couple of leaps sprinkled into the process. But they were leaps that my teacher knew that I was ready for, even though I wasn't quite aware of it yet. This story is also about paralyzing fear. *And how sometimes, sometimes, the very things we are afraid of are areas where we have a gift, a talent, an affinity or skill.*

In this case my fear was definitely based in illusion. Have you ever been nervous or fearful about trying something new, and later, after trying it, you discovered that it was easy or fun or not scary at all? What about learning to walk, ride a bike or swim?

We all have had experiences of overcoming fear. Remembering them brings us the empowerment of knowing that we have done it before, *and we can do it again.*

This story is also about how that first step of signing up for an introductory acting class to overcome shyness opened doorway after doorway and led me to other joyful things that I otherwise might never have discovered or experienced.

I retired from professional acting in 1986. I enjoyed it and learned from the gifts it brought my way. It was a vehicle that lead me to more joy. It was the connector from the extremely shy person who couldn't talk to anyone to becoming a workshop leader, mental health educator and consultant. It helped me become a better and more confident communicator. It helped me learn to take the genuineness that was inside me and express it in the world. It helped me to learn how to be more authentic as a person—instead of hiding behind a wall of fear.

Take that first step. Taking baby steps really works. That's how this book finally got completed! That's how my husband and I have created a happy life together. Prioritize your time to make space for the new and wonderful activity, project, or person in your life.

CHAPTER 9

GETTING WHERE YOU
WANT TO GO

A journey of 1000 miles
begins with a single step.

—Lao-Tsu—

Once you know what makes you happy, it's time to take action. The next couple of chapters will give you information that separates the doers from the perpetual dreamers (the Walter Mittys). In other words, though being a dreamer is an *important* part in the whole process of creating joy and happiness, unfortunately, sometimes those dreams remain just that: dreams. The missing ingredient is action—taking steps, even baby steps, toward making that dream a reality in your life.

I have found for myself that whenever I am experiencing fear about trying something new, baby steps help me to stay on track because I don't overwhelm myself with too much too soon.

Pat yourself on the back with each step in your Joy Journal to track the success of your journey and empower the action you are taking.

For some people, it can be easy to let this part slide, because *whenever you are adding something new to your life, you have to prioritize your time in order to make a place for it.*

Prioritization was one of the biggest challenges I had to deal with in completing this book, as an example. Saying that I was too busy was an easy "out" to not setting aside the time. In fact, I had written over half of this book and did not work on it for over a year, telling myself that I didn't have the time. The truth is, I would have had the time if I had worked it into my schedule. I found that one to two mornings a week for an hour or two was an easy way to consistently work on it to completion. When I put things off till the evening, I was usually not up for it because I had already used a lot of energy in the activity of the day. Not prioritizing is a *very* easy way to procrastinate.

A friend of mine asked me about how my book was coming, and when I told him that I didn't have the time to work on it, his reply was,

"Last time I checked there were still 24 hours in a day."

This was an eye-opener for me, because it shattered my excuse and my illusion that there was less time available to me. Once I worked it into my schedule, *I found that I still had the time to do everything else that I was doing before!* Funny how that works!

The whole process of action toward your dreams is much easier and more manageable if you set realistic goals and create a flexible timeline in easy steps. One of the biggest sabotages I have experienced in my goal-setting is that, in my passion and excitement, I created timelines that were unrealistic. I wanted to get there FAST. But that set me up for failure when I did not reach those unrealistic deadlines I had set for myself. Then I would get discouraged and quit. I was my own saboteur! I did this several times on the writing of this book. When I finally became much more flexible with my plan, then I started seeing progress.

The important thing to remember with goal-setting is that the goals themselves are only the *vehicles* to help get you moving into the *process.* After all, it really is the journey, not the destination, where our happiness lies. Once we meet our goals, what do we do? We come up with others.

Once I reached my goal as a professional actress of working with some of the best actors in the world at one of the best theatres in the world, that accomplished, I wanted to move on to something else that would bring me fulfillment. What I had learned and the growth I had experienced prepared me for the next step, or doorway, which would bring me another wave of fulfillment.

I started teaching workshops to share what I had learned with others. My acting career helped transform a shy, reclusive person into one who could get up in front of a group of people and enjoy it. It also helped me become a more effective communicator, so that my message could be understood and heard by my audience. And once I had fulfilling, successful experiences doing workshops, I then wanted to write this book.

Don't get stuck in your goals thinking that their attainment is where you will finally achieve happiness forever, amen. It is the *journey,* the *process,* where the joy is. In many parts of the world today, particularly in western culture, producing a product or reaching that destination is what is prized (not the process), but that makes for whole cultures of people who are driven, stressed and *not* experiencing happiness in daily life!

The quote by Mahatma Gandhi at the beginning of Chapter Fifteen, *"There is more to life than increasing its speed,"* is so true. Did he achieve a lot in his life? How about helping a whole country reach independence and establish its own government, and, in the process, teach the whole world about love in action! It wasn't until I relaxed with the process of this book (without being driven) that I started enjoying every writing session and found the happiness right in front of me. And it is gravy to know that the process may lead you to other joyful things that you cannot even imagine at this point.

I have made some disclaimers about goals, but they are still an effective means of beginning the journey, taking action, and keeping us on track with our dreams.

Henry David Thoreau said,

"If you have built castles in the air, your work need not be lost; that is where they should be. Now put the foundations under them."

TOOL #6

Monthly Goal Worksheet

Use this worksheet to help you stay on track with your process. Review this worksheet, from time to time, to see if your timeline (as planned out here) is realistic and workable. **Make adjustments with timelines whenever they are needed.** *For a long-term project, you will need to create another sheet each month. It is hard before you begin the process to know what is a good, easy level of activity to keep the process workable. As you grow and change, your goals may also change.* **Be flexible and willing to even change the goal to fit who you are.** *This worksheet is a way of saying, "I commit to taking action in this process for that which brings me happiness."*

What is the activity, career, hobby or thing, etc. that is the focus of the goal sheet?

*Step(s) I can take **this week** toward this goal:*

*Step(s) I can take **next week** toward this goal:*

*Steps I can take **this month** toward this goal:*

*Signed*_____*Date*_____

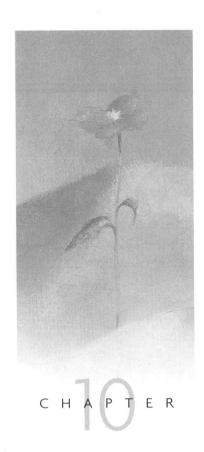

CHAPTER 10

CHANGE HAPPENS

All is flux, nothing stays still.
—Heraclitus—

Happiness and fulfillment are not things that, once we've experienced them, we never have to *create* them again. The word *create* is important here, because the truth of it is, if you have experienced happiness, *you* have created it or brought it into your life through your choices, awareness and perceptions. You probably have already discovered that once you attain happiness and fulfillment in something, you do not remain that way forever. We change. What we want changes. Our jobs change. Our interests change. *Happiness and fulfillment is a process.*

We can depend on it: Change happens. But change is the sign of growth and expansion of who we are, and that is a good thing.

As you grow and change, your goals may change or you may expand your definition of an activity that brings you happiness. As an example, you may have been doing work that has always been good and satisfying for you, but you are no longer finding it as fulfilling as you used to. You have changed in your relation to your work. What has changed? Your attitude? Your interest? Have you discovered another kind of work that you enjoy more?

Many people think that when they no longer find fulfillment in something, they need to replace it. *But that is not always what is needed.* It might be that your *perception* of the work has changed, therefore affecting your enjoyment of it. Or it might be that, indeed, another type of work might be what is needed.

When you reach a goal, what happens? You come up with another one. Ideally our visions and goals help to bring us into the process of living by focusing our energy on what makes us happy. I mentioned in an earlier chapter, what is so often misunderstood about happiness is the belief that we do not attain that happiness and fulfillment until we reach the goal. Happiness and fulfillment is *in the journey.* The goal is really only a vehicle to bring us into the process of *living* our joy.

CHAPTER 11

BUMPS IN THE ROAD

Live as if you were to die tomorrow.
Learn as if you were to live forever.
—M.K. Gandhi—

Bumps in the road are an inevitable part of life. Our bumps can come from many different sources. Falling down is how we learned to walk, after all, so a life without a stumble here and there is a life that is probably controlled by fear without many steps being taken.

Many bumps we encounter can be of our own making—products of our own free will. This chapter will cover those bumps in the road that many people experience at one time or another with suggestions on how to help make the journey smoother.

Procrastination

Procrastination is a bump in the road that we put there ourselves. But why do we procrastinate? Why do we put things off that make us happy? There can be many different reasons, but, generally speaking, these reasons can usually be boiled down to this: the fear of failure in one way or another. Unless you deal with it, fear can derail your dreams altogether. I know, because my procrastination nearly kept this book from being completed. Poor planning of our time and not prioritizing to fit an activity or thing into our lives is an easy way to avoid trying and, therefore, risking failure.

Working more balance into our schedules is a good way to deal with the tendency to procrastinate.

Perfectionism

Perfectionism is usually created by fear, as well, and can result in procrastination. Behind my own perfectionism lurked a fear of failure, because I feared that I wasn't good enough, that I didn't have what it would take to successfully complete the task/project/challenge. I also feared that if I tried and messed up that I would experience hardship (the hardship usually created by me in my self-criticism).

Have you ever been afraid that if you *unintentionally* made a mistake that you would experience hardship or punishment?

What finally helped me get over my perfectionism was the realization that *who I am transcends what I do.* When I have messed up in my life, it wasn't intentional. And I was very distressed if it caused difficulty for anyone else. But what I did with that was to punish myself harshly (by beating myself up mentally) whenever I made a mistake. I attacked my worth as a person, my goodness as a person. And I also feared that the world would punish me as harshly as I punished myself. I confused the mistake with *who* I was, saying to myself things like, "You're a big mess-up. You can't do anything right! Who did you think you were fooling by trying to do this!" Looking back on it, it was sad that I had abused myself so.

One day, years ago, I had a very humbling experience. I was thinking about how hard I was on myself, and I had this realization: In my mind, I saw the image of a baby trying to learn to walk, and every time it stumbled or fell, I kicked it. It was horrifying. That baby represented me, and what that image in my mind showed me was how sad and painful what I was doing to myself really was. We are all learning to walk in different ways at different times. We will stumble here and there to figure out how to do it. I was cruelly kicking myself whenever I stumbled. It showed me how damaging and inappropriate I was being with myself.

Forgiving ourselves is as important as forgiving others. Being compassionate with ourselves when we make a mistake can also help us be more compassionate with others when they stumble, as well.

What I am saying here is not intended to be misused as an excuse. If you are aware of what you are doing and its possible effects, and you do it anyway, it is *not* a mistake. It might be an inappropriate choice, but it didn't happen innocently.

Mistakes will happen. It's a part of life. Have you ever looked at a difficult situation, and seen how the choices you made created it? Ideally, you learn from it, clean up the mess, if there is one (by apologizing to those it affected), and move on, *being careful not to repeat it.*

The Free Will of Others

Bumps in the road can also happen as a result of the free will of others—not because they are trying to block you, but because what someone else wants just happens to get in the way of what you want. As an example, have you ever applied for a job that you really wanted and you didn't get it? The interviewer's choice for the job was not in line with what you wanted.

We cannot control the free will of others. And, beyond your understanding of the job and what it really entailed, it may not have been the best thing for you. That person (or God/Creator/Universe working through that person) could very well have done you a favor, because there may have been something much better waiting for you. In other instances where what you want and what someone else wants doesn't mesh, you can try negotiating something that will work for everybody. Negotiation will be dealt with in the chapter, "Compassionate Communication".

Fear

As mentioned earlier in this chapter, fear is an obstacle that can prevent us from realizing our dreams or experiencing sustained happiness, if we let it control us. Fear has had a function in our lives when we were younger—to keep us or others safe. Fear made us aware of potential dangers, like crossing a busy street or falling from a high place. Fear, of course, can still serve to warn us of dangers, but, for most of us, much of what we fear in our adult lives is based in illusion.

As an example, survey after survey shows that the number one fear most people have is the fear of getting up in front of a group of people. This really is an illusory fear. You are in a very safe place when you are in front of a group of people (unless you are a standup comedian or a politician!). Think back. Have you ever observed a performance or a speech in which the speaker blanked out or the actor lost a line? Probably. How did you respond? Did you get up and shout insults? Did anyone else? Did you think, "Gee, what a mess-up!" No, you probably had very supportive thoughts and concern for the presenter, and when they picked it back up, you were relieved. Audiences really are very supportive and understanding. When you give yourself a chance to experience getting up in front of groups, you train that part of yourself that was fearful that you *can* do it and that it is not dangerous.

Persistence or Bulldozing?

When you encounter a bump in the road, sometimes looking for another way to do what you have been doing might be helpful. If you are wanting to open a door, and it is closed, it may take a couple of tries to find the right key. In other words, don't quit just because your first try at something doesn't bring the results you had hoped for. Try some more and look for other ways to do it. Persistence *can* be important. Don't give up too soon before you have given alternative ways a try.

I learned that, many times, persistence and resilience were needed if I wanted to work as an actor. In fact, one director thanked me for my persistence in trying to contact him. He had a very busy schedule, and the situation called for persistence on my part in order to open that door of opportunity.

The previous paragraph brings us to this razor's edge issue. *Where do you draw the line between persistence and stubbornly trying to open a door that was not meant for you to open?* Those with a strong will can repeatedly throw themselves up against a brick wall or a locked door. Have you ever gotten what you wanted and found out that it wasn't something you wanted after all? Sometimes we don't know (in our limited perspective of the big picture) all of what is best for us, and a door remains closed for a good reason. And as Hamlet said, there is more at work, Horatio, than we can imagine.

So, how do you know the difference between forcing something to happen (or bulldozing) and healthy, appropriate persistence? If you are someone who usually gives up after try-ing to contact someone once or twice, then persistence is probably needed. If you are someone who will try to bulldoze to get what you want, be sensitive to the process of when no is NO.

Here is something that works for me: If I have used several ways of trying to make something work (and I have been persist-ent), and the door still has not opened, then I stop to look at the situation more closely. I usually try to find someone who has had experience with it and ask him or her for any tips that might be helpful. For instance, when I was an actor, I found directors were very helpful in telling me what they look for in the audition process.

If I am still not opening a door, then I have a talk with the deeper levels of my awareness. I check to see if I am limiting what the opportunity might look like. The doorway may be packaged in a way that I can't see it because I am expecting it to look like something else. Sometimes, if I am not sure about whether a doorway is meant for me, asking for things to be clearer helps. "If this is not the best thing for me, if this is not for the highest good, please close this door completely so that it will be clear that it is not for me." I don't know about you, but there have been times when I have looked back and thanked the whole universe for not allowing that door to be opened!

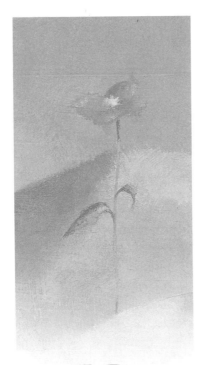

CHAPTER 12

BOUNCING BACK

Love. . .
It surrounds every being and extends slowly
to embrace all that shall be.
—Kahlil Gibran—

We all make mistakes (or even fall flat on our faces), and we will continue to make mistakes (hopefully different ones, not the same ones!). Mistakes will happen and what we *do* about the mistakes is important. Let's say a mistake inconveniences or causes distress for another. I'm not at all a happy camper when I have created difficulty for another through a mistake or miscommunication I have made, and the most immediate thing I have learned to do as an adult is damage control.

Apologies are a way to create or at least begin a healing when one has fallen down and made things hard for someone else. I have found in my life that apologies are necessary where I have responsibility and/or had a part in a mistake or miscommunication. Even lack of clarity in communication can create a situation where an apology is needed. It takes strength not weakness to make a real or genuine apology. People who need to be right (or are fearful of being wrong) or are acting out of insecurity have a very hard time making an apology.

What I meant earlier by a *real* or *genuine* apology is one that has no ego in it. No justifications first about why you couldn't help it. A REAL apology goes something like this:

"I am sorry (not 'I apologize') for _____ that had the effect or caused_____. I will do the best I can not to do this again."

An example could be:

"I'm sorry for being late and caused you to have to wait. I'll do everything I can to be on time and not be late for one of our appointments again."

If it involves someone close to you, then asking for forgiveness is also an important part.

If you find that you keep making similar mistakes around the same kinds of issues, then you need to pay attention. For instance, you may keep missing deadlines because you procrastinate. This is a pattern that shows you something that needs attention in your life—behavior that needs to be acknowledged and replaced, otherwise you will find yourself on that treadmill creating dramas again and again.

Back to apologies. I was having a conversation with someone the other day about apologies, and he was saying that if *not* doing something that one had agreed to do does not cause difficulty for the other person, then an apology is not needed. I disagree with this thinking, because if I agree to something and then don't do it (for whatever reason), even if it does not *seemingly* cause inconvenience or difficulty for another, I will never know if I don't acknowledge the slip-up and apologize. It's a relief when I do apologize and find that my slip-up did not create difficulty for another.

The other person will know by your apology that you respect them and the agreement with your consideration.

We have nothing to lose by apologizing for a slip-up or a mistake, even though our ego may tell us differently. People learn more about you by *observing* you than by anything else, and heartfelt apologies show strength of character. I know I have admiration for someone who acts with that kind of impeccability.

Let's say you find that you did do something inadvertently that caused difficulty for another. An apology is a beginning. The next thing is to forgive yourself for messing up.

Feeling shame and guilt as a result of beating yourself up over making a mistake is very destructive to happiness. Dive back into activity—don't sit around licking your wounds or fearing future mess-ups. We're human, and we will mess up again.

The important thing I have had to remember is that the mistake is not *who* I am, and that to bounce back and get moving again is strength and is worthy of the best of me. I admire those who do this, and I feel good myself when I have gotten up, dusted myself off, and started *living* again.

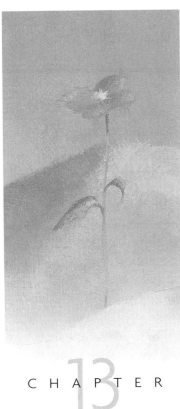

CHAPTER 13

ATTITUDE IS A CHOICE

Human beings, by changing the inner attitudes of their minds,
can change the outer aspects of their lives.

–William James–

Pain is a part of life and can be a bump in the road—whether it be emotional or physical pain. I have a dear friend who experiences a great deal of physical pain but does not allow the "bumps" to become serious potholes in her life. There is a difference between pain and suffering.

Physical pain is a part of life because it is there for a reason. Our bodies are trying to tell us that something needs our attention. Chronic conditions or diseases can require management and creativity in finding ways to function with them.

My dear friend that I mentioned earlier lives with a condition in which she has to deal with chronic pain. She has found ways to manage the pain the best she can, and she has also chosen to focus on what she *can* do instead of what she *cannot* do. If she had given in to focusing on what she cannot do, then her pain would become suffering. To know this remarkable woman is to know a happy and very loving person.

I have been dense at times in my life by not listening to what my body through physical pain was trying to tell me. One such message from my body was: "You are doing too much. Slow down!" And I did not heed the call and became sick. Have you ever done too much work or kept yourself too busy, and your body finally got your full attention to it's run-down immune system by getting the flu? Hmmm. Self-created bump in the road. I've had to learn to pay attention, to know my body and what it needs. For me that means backing off from foods that I know don't make me feel good (and eating those that do make me feel good), not working into the wee hours of the morning, and also not overdoing it with exercise. This 50-something body loves exercise, but not too much and not the wrong kind. My back and joints let me know, and I have learned through trial and error not to go there.

Earlier in this chapter I mentioned emotional pain. An example of this type of pain is grief. Grief is a natural response to the death or loss of a person, animal or way of life that we love.

There is a hole in one's life, and it hurts. There is a natural process to grief, and many books have been written about it. That natural process becomes suffering, however, when, years later, that person is still grieving, sad, and desolate. What I'm talking about here is not a momentary missing or sadness that may surface with a memory of someone who is gone. I'm referring to a continuous pall of grief that hangs like a shroud over daily experience years after the loss. That is suffering. In a situation like that, for instance, happiness cannot thrive.

Pain happens and so does change, but it is what we do with what happens in our lives that makes the difference. Even in the midst of life with a large spectrum of things that can be experienced, happiness can be there. Happiness is always right in front of us—waiting to be seen and experienced moment to moment. It is an ever present potential.

CHAPTER 14

THE MAGIC OF LAUGHTER

Laughter is the sun that drives winter
from the human face.

−Victor Hugo−

There's no getting around it: Laughter is fun. Most of us know that laughter is good for us, and it is a great stress-buster. Humor can help us problem-solve and work through difficulty by showing the absurdity in a situation or drama. Laughing can give us some "distance" so that we can better see the bigger picture. Being able to laugh at ourselves is a sign of strength.

Employers hire me to do my Humor in the Workplace staff and professional development seminars because they want employees to enjoy their work. Employers also know that laughter enhances productivity, creativity and raises morale. Humor can build teams by dissolving barriers to accessibility and understanding.

When people are asked what the most important quality is that they look for in a relationship or mate, usually the number one answer is a sense of humor. The reason for that may be because laughter makes life easier and more *livable,* and it *is* fun to laugh! Relationships of all kinds (friendships, family, partnerships, professional relationships, etc.) benefit from humor and laughter. One of the things I enjoy and appreciate about my own family is their sense of humor.

My husband and I love to be silly and playful. By finding ways to make each other laugh we bring bright moments of fun into our lives.

Humor, however, can sometimes have the opposite effect if it is not appropriate. Passive-aggressive humor, for instance, is not funny. Wisecracks and sarcasm are not humor in the positive sense; they are negative and destructive. Sarcasm is defined by the *Merriam-Webster Online Dictionary as "a sharp or often satirical or ironic utterance designed to cut or give pain. . ." Know the intent behind your humor.

---

*By permission. From the *Merriam-Webster Online Dictionary* ©2005 by Merriam-Webster, Incorporated (www.Merriam-Webster.com).

Laughter and humor used appropriately has many, many benefits. Here is my list:

- Laughter creates positive connections among people and facilitates communication and understanding.
- Humor develops mental flexibility.
- Humor is effective in problem-solving.
- Humor and laughter make life fun and joyful.
- Laughter builds teams.
- Laughter raises morale in the workplace and creates a more positive atmosphere.
- Humor and laughter makes difficulties easier to work through and is a great stress-buster.

Abraham Lincoln was right—*"Laughter is the universal evergreen of life."* Look for opportunities to laugh everyday!

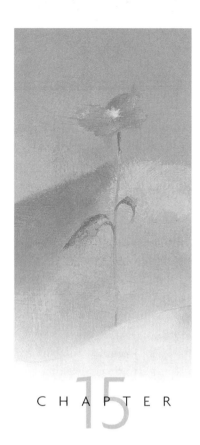

CHAPTER 15

THE SPEED OF LIFE

There is more to life than increasing its speed.
—M.K. Gandhi—

No one on his deathbed says, "Darn, I wish I could have worked one more day!" If people have regrets at the end of their lives, they are usually, "I wish I had said 'I love you' more." or "I wish I had been kinder, more compassionate." or "I wish I had taken the time to do the things that made me happy." Living at the speed of life means slowing down enough to *listen*. Those regrets that people usually experience at the end of their lives *are promptings that have been there throughout their lives that they have ignored*.

The work ethic in the U.S. is very strong. Many Americans are too driven and engage their minds almost exclusively with work and careers. Relationships suffer when all of our focus is taken up by our work.

Even if a person dislikes his work, he may spend a lot of time when he's not there thinking about how much he dislikes it and how much he would like to do something else. But if some time is taken *to just listen* for ideas or promptings on how the job could be made better or more enjoyable, a shift might happen in the perception and experience of the work.

"Slow myself down to listen to who or what?" you may ask. Well, my answer would be many voices and yet one voice: That still, small voice within, or the same situation that presents itself to you over and over, or doors opening or closing, or what your child is saying with his behavior.

Slowing down to the speed of life means slowing ourselves down enough to pull ourselves out of *autopilot*—out of that dead end routine, out of behaviors and ways of thinking that no longer work for us, out of reactions that create separation instead of unity.

Slowing down to the speed of life means *waking up*, being fully alive right now, knowing that in every moment resides that choice to be awake. As used in this chapter, being asleep means ignoring those promptings of our hearts until they become regrets.

I have found that what I need to know is within me and spoken though Creation all around me. Life is filled with miracles and magic, but unless I am listening and watching, even the miracles will be missed.

Something I have found refreshing is to just sit quietly for a few minutes and listen to the silence or my heart beating. I have found contemplative walks to be a wonderful time to get creative ideas. Being out in nature is a way that many people find the silence and peace to listen.

Slowing down also means waking up to the wonder of life again. Listening to your heart when it says, "take a break, play, be silly!" But it's so easy to say, "I don't have the time." And it's so easy to see another day of life fly by without joy.

Here's a suggestion: Take a walk after dark sometime in your neighborhood—if it's a safe residential neighborhood. As you walk by, notice how many houses have the light of the television illuminating a room. Or notice if a stereo is blasting away. Notice all the things that people do to keep them occupied and asleep. Could any of those homes be yours? Having stuff coming at us all the time is an easy way to avoid being alive. Some people even wake up to the television and go to sleep in front of it. Daily routines can become ruts that distract from the promptings of our hearts or the still, small voice within.

When we slow down we can more clearly see things that need attention in our lives. It might be that a relationship or friendship needs some processing time—time to talk things over and check in with how things are going and what might be needed to bring more joy into it. What might need attention is your body—needing exercise or a healthy diet. You might discover, if you listen, that you really need to take a vacation. You might be reminded to make a phone call or write a letter that you've been putting off. When you really listen, promptings can become fulfilling action instead of regrets.

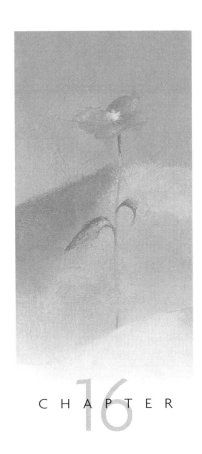

CHAPTER 16

CREATIVITY AND PLAY

Wooohooooo!
–Cambo the Clown–

Creativity and play can be the source of much happiness in life. When leading my creativity and play workshops, I ask at the beginning, "How many of you think of yourselves as being creative?" Usually, out of a whole room full of people, only a few will raise their hands. I believe that *everyone* is a creative person, but from my experience in leading these workshops, what usually limits someone in thinking about being creative is the definition of creativity being used, one that puts creativity into a limited compartment.

Actually, creativity can be found in just about everything we do, if we allow ourselves to be aware of it.

Here are just a few ways that we use creativity in our daily lives:

- Gardening
- Problem-solving
- Cooking
- Writing letters, correspondences
- Home decorating
- Choosing the clothes and colors to wear each day
- Romance
- Singing
- Organizing
- Play
- Crafts
- Drawing/painting
- Styling one's hair
- Parenting
- Humor
- Dancing

The list can go on and on. The key is awareness. In any given moment, we are making a choice, and the more aware we are of making that choice, the more creative we are. Play is a very pure form of creativity. There is usually no product to have expectations about, and we play just for the joy of it. In our household, our cats have been excellent teachers for us in the joy of play. Being silly can give me a great energy boost in the middle of the day!

Problem-solving is a very practical and high level use of creativity. It helps us find common ground with others and create more ease in life.

When I've asked, many people tell me they believe that creativity is limited to the arts, like painting, playing a musical instrument, singing, acting, dancing or creative writing. That is usually why most people don't think of themselves as creative, but once they expand that definition in their minds and then shift their perceptions, they can begin to see that, yes, they are creative! Abundantly creative, I would say. Creative uses of our minds can simply be finding different ways of perceiving things or different ways of doing things. An awareness of how much we use creativity in daily life brings more meaning, happiness and joy!

As I mentioned earlier, play is a form of creativity that is easy and can create much happiness. Here is a list of just a few playful activities:

- Playing with your pets
- Singing a silly song
- Playing cards or board games
- Skipping
- Charades and other group or party games
- Free-form dancing to music at home
- Blowing bubbles
- Playing a kazoo

- Coloring

- Talking in character voices

- Playing drums or bongos

- Whistling

- Making funny faces

- Lip-sinking to your favorite song

- Clowning around with silly clothing
  and props

Because of all the happy benefits we receive from play, it's time to get serious about being silly!

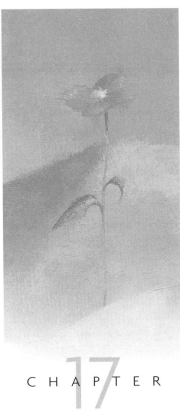

CHAPTER 17

THINKING THE BEST OF OTHERS

Life appears to me to be too short to be spent in
nursing animosity or registering wrong.
–Charlotte Brontë–
Jane Eyre

The Golden Rule, "Do unto others as you would have them do unto you," shows up in some form as a common thread in almost every major world philosophy or spiritual tradition. I feel at peace with myself when I appropriately *give* what I would like to receive from others, and that giving of respect, consideration, and love makes me happy.

Thinking the best of others has been something that I've had to train myself to do over the years. Before that self-training, I was regularly projecting negative intent onto others, and it was so much a part of my perceptual reality that I didn't know I was doing it. Because of that, I had a bit of a chip on my shoulder. I came to realize, though, that whenever I was having a negative thought about someone, I was usually not thinking the best of him or her.

In most of our lives, *most* of the time, people aren't out to have negative effects on others. Of course, there are exceptions, and, hopefully, you will be well aware when you are encountering one. If you know that the bull will charge, *don't stand in front of it.*

People sometimes act badly because they were "raised by wolves" and are not very good at communicating, or they may be reacting defensively, incorrectly projecting that there is a threat coming from you. To illustrate dealing with projecting negative intent onto others (or not thinking the best of others), here is an example of an intrapersonal dialog:

"Joe is trying to make things hard for me."

"What's going on with you to have a thought like that about Joe?"

"Because he was inconsiderate and that made more work for me."

"How do you know that he is trying to be inconsiderate or create more work for you?

"I just know."

"How can you know what he is thinking?

Are you an accomplished mind reader?"

"I just don't trust him, that's all."

"Why don't you trust him?"

"Because it has happened to me before."

"What?"

"In another situation, I had to clean up a mess that he made at work."

"When that happened before, did you talk to him about it?"

"No. He knew that it would make my job harder."

"Really. Have you ever inconvenienced someone or made things harder for that person without realizing it?

"Yes."

"How did you know?"

"It got back to me."

"Would you have known if it had not gotten back to you?"

"No."

"Okay. Why are you thinking the worst of Joe? You can't know what he is thinking, and he is probably not even aware that he has done something that has had this effect. Casually talk to him about it and assume the best of him in your communication (that he is not aware that he has made things difficult for you)."

I have learned from experience that I cannot really know someone else's intent or what they are thinking unless they tell me. I have also learned as an adult that, if my feelings are hurt, the other person usually has no awareness that it would effect me that way.

It is rare for people to intentionally want to have any kind of negative effect on others. Naturally, one should heed one's intuition when it signals caution or, for instance, avoid extreme situations like walking down a dark alley at midnight!

Looking at the world scene, I'm sure you can think of dramatic situations where there actually was a negative intent behind an action, but what I am talking about here is the type of contact and day-to-day experiences most of us have. Also, on a day when we are not feeling at our best, we may be overly sensitive to things that wouldn't negatively affect us on a good day. But that has more to do with self-awareness than it has to do with anyone who might have ruffled our feathers.

I find that a few hours alone (or sleeping on it) and keeping the "ruffle" to myself allows me to get things in perspective, and then I am able to see that, many times, it was really just me.

Dragging someone through your personal drama or issue can be a way to alienate people and lose friends. And, gosh, when that happens it can sure squelch one's happiness!

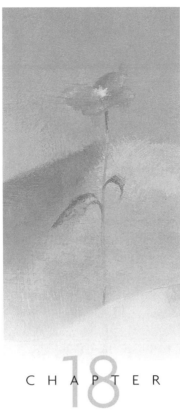

C H A P T E R 18

COMPASSIONATE
COMMUNICATION

Be the change you want to see in the world.
—M.K. Gandhi—

Communication is one of the most important factors in creating happiness in our lives. I talked about *intrapersonal* communication in the early part of this book, because it forms the *foundation* for happiness. There is another kind of communication that goes hand-in-hand with intrapersonal communication and that is our communication with others, *interpersonal* communication. *Everything* we experience in our lives involves relationships—they may be close personal ones or they may be the relationships we have with our co-workers, friends, or the people standing next to us at the bus stop.

Compassionate communication is about finding a way to communicate in any given exchange with respect and loving intent. When I say loving intent, I am not referring to only the romantic kind of love. In Chapter Five I wrote about the many different kinds of love and how inclusive love is. With the foundation of compassion for any communication, one can create more unity in daily living. Unity brings peace and happiness.

Unity as used here does not mean agreement, it means working in understanding of a common vision. That common vision might be to create a beautiful community park for all to enjoy or to work on a website with a designer to develop the best possible tool for your dream. A common vision between you and the grocery clerk, for instance, may be as simple as getting your items checked out in the grocery line easily and enjoyably.

Humans have free will, and conflicts will arise from time to time. Having a happy life doesn't mean a life without conflict, but having the ability to *cope* well with conflict when it does come up makes for a happier life. Sometimes, as discussed in the chapter, "Bumps in the Road," our free will and the free will of others might seemingly be at odds. A compassionate communication can result in a mutual awareness that neither party has negative intent at all, just paths of action bumping into one another. Sometimes that awareness is all that is needed to open the door to finding an easy solution that resolves the difficulty. Communication is the key to finding something that works. Sometimes, however, what works may be to simply agree to disagree.

Working on an agreement requires negotiation and possibly even compromise. Compromise has a negative connotation for some, but I have found that compromising a bit sometimes brings the unreachable and grandiose into the realm of realistic possibility.

Let's look at what can go into developing a compassionate communication:

1) Have an intent to communicate with respect and love.

2) Look for some kind of commonality (it may be the common vision) instead of looking at the differences.

3) Come up with some options or ideas to consider that seem workable to you.

4) Look to negotiation to find something that will work for everyone.

There will be times in our lives when an agreement or compact has not been honored or a problem keeps coming up with someone. Maybe someone missed an important appointment with you or someone is doing something that makes things harder for you. Particularly, if it is *more* than just an isolated instance, it is important to communicate about it. In order to approach it in a way that will, hopefully, pave the way for a positive interaction, what is required is a *compassionate* confrontation.

A compassionate confrontation is also a communication with the intent to communicate with respect and love. Communicating with compassion means here that you are approaching a problem *thinking* the best of others, and *communicating* in a way that clearly shows you are thinking the best of them. This also helps them to save face and to *hear* what you are communicating without getting defensive. There is a caveat here: There are some people in the world who will get defensive and feel threatened even with a compassionate communication like this, but that is not something you have control over.

We only have control over our own reactions, not those of others. So there is always that possibility that no matter how lovingly we communicate, it might not be received well. That is the risk in all communications, BUT we can do everything we know to do to make it respectful, loving and compassionate. Always seek to do no harm.

Sometimes though, even with the best intentions, your compassionate confrontation may not convey the same meaning that you intended. I have even apologized and clarified for a compassionate confrontation that I have made if I see that I could have been clearer or I realize my good intentions were misunderstood.

What would a compassionate confrontation look like? Well, there is no promise with any communication that if you follow certain steps you will be successful. Communication is a very dynamic thing because of the free will of everyone involved, which can bring unpredictability to things. There is no magic communication system. Having said all of that, to help you think through your communication in advance and make it as compassionate as possible, here are some things to remember:

1) Remember that the underlying intent is communicating with compassion and respect.

2) Think the best of others.

3) Try putting yourself in their shoes, and try to see what their actions might mean to *them.*

4) Communicate in a way that they will know that you are thinking the best of them.

5) Separate the behavior from the person in your communication. We are not our behavior; we are much more than that. In other words, if someone is behaving badly, that does not make him/her a bad person.

Here are some examples of compassionate confrontations I have made.

Someone missed an appointment with me and I waited 30 minutes and didn't receive any communication:

> *I know life can get really busy and sometimes chaotic, and it can be easy to overlook details. We had an appointment on _____, and I'm calling to make sure everything is okay and to reschedule our meeting.*

To an "old-school" business associate who has repeatedly used some humor around me that I don't appreciate and find inappropriate:

> *You're not the sort of person who would deliberately try to make me uncomfortable, but that's what happens when you tell (ethnic, religious, political) jokes. I'd appreciate it a lot if you'd hold off on that sort of humor when we're together. I would enjoy hearing more about your amazing travels anyway.*

These are given only as *ideas* of what a compassionate confrontation might look like.

Of all the tools in this book, communication (both intrapersonal and interpersonal) is probably the most powerful in creating happiness. By using compassionate communication with *ourselves* we empower the positive within us and create that important foundation for happiness. In compassionate communication with *others,* we are able to *live* the Golden Rule by treating others with the respect and love that we would like for ourselves. Think of the possibilities for unity and peace in our world! It must always begin with ourselves: We must *live* what it is we want to see in the world.

CHAPTER 19

YOU ARE NOT ALONE

I believe a leaf of grass is no less than
the journeywork of the stars.
—Walt Whitman—

Slowing down to the speed of life has given me more fulfillment and happiness, because I can more clearly see *meaning* in my daily life and see the partnership that I have with the Divine in the unfolding of my experience. I have found that the Creator through Creation is constantly trying to help me and is doing everything possible to facilitate my happiness, but it is a *partnership*. Unless I take steps toward my dreams (that free will thing), it's hard for the Universe to help me.

Years ago I gave up that notion that God is a vengeful god who judges, smites and punishes. Punishment is human stuff, and God/Creator isn't human. Thank god. I have been my greatest punisher. Unconditional love and forgiveness, in my view, is what is Divine, and we can strive to express the Divine in us in that way. God *is* love.

All life is interconnected. What we do and even think has an effect in this world. Mystics have been saying this for thousands of years. My high school biology teacher once told us that we are made of stardust. I have never forgotten that because it made such an impression on me and brought hope to my heart. The idea that we are all a part of a greater whole rang true for me. We are not alone because what we are is magic, stardust.

With that awareness, it makes the free will I have been given a responsibility that I need to respect and use well. Our choices can open doors and help us create our lives along with the help of a supportive Universe made from Love.

ABOUT THE AUTHOR

Mary Claire O'Neal lives with her husband, Cam (a professional clown), and their cat, Willie (also a clown), in the green, rolling hills of central Kentucky. She has a communication consulting business and has been teaching workshops in the art of effective and meaningful communication, happiness, humor, attitude, presentation skills, and creativity for nearly twenty years. Her work experience includes Equity actor, mental health educator, arts consultant, and teacher/counselor working with kids at risk and/or with behavioral disorders. Mary Claire offers services as a keynote speaker, consultant, coach, and teacher of workshops and classes. She is a member of the National Speakers' Association.

Visit her website at:
www.maryclaireoneal.com

ORDER FORM

To order more copies of this book by phone:

River Birch Publishing, LLC
P.O. Box 23198
Lexington, KY 40523-3198

(859) 272-2515

OR

Order online at:

www.maryclaireoneal.com

Mastercard and Visa accepted

NOTES